Hello!
I am a bee.

Bees are busy. One bee can visit up to 1,500 flowers in a single day!

Bees have a special body part called a "proboscis".

I use my proboscis like a straw to suck up nectar from flowers.

Bees have two sets of wings.

That's a total of 4 wings all together.

When bees visit flowers to collect nectar, pollen sticks to their bodies and gets put onto other flowers.

A group of bees is called a "colony".

Small colonies have a few hundred bees. Big ones have tens of thousands!

Some bees have "pollen baskets" on their hind legs.

They bring the pollen to other worker bees who will store and use it as food for the colony.

Bees have five eyes!

They have two big compound eyes and three smaller eyes on top of their head.

Bees usually live for just a few weeks to several months.

However, queen honeybees can live for several years.

Each hive has only one queen bee. Her main job is to lay eggs to create more bees.

I can lay up to 2000 eggs in one day.

The worker bees in the hive take care of the queen bee and feed her "royal jelly" to help her grow and stay healthy.

Bees communicate with each other by dancing!

The "waggle dance" shows other bees where to find food.

The "queen dance" lets other bees know where the queen is.

When bees are born they don't know how to make honey. They learn from older bees in the hive.

When a bee returns to the hive, it tells the other bees where to find food.

Bees can recognize landmarks and use the position of the sun to find their way.

Honeybee hives are made up of six-sided cells called "honeycombs".

In the honeycombs bees store their food, raise baby bees, and even save up their extra honey .

Bee hives can be found in many different places, like trees, hollow logs, or even man-made beehives.

Bees work hard to keep their hive clean and free from trash and pests.

They use their hairy "antennae" to help them sense different scents.

www.ingramcontent.com/pod-product-compliance
Lightning Source LLC
Chambersburg PA
CBHW041500120626

46547CB00003B/491